INTRODUCTION

Since the introduction of the "How to Teach......" series of sport has changed, particularly as a result of "open" at become more popular with children, offering the sch... .... opportunity to educate children through a most satisfying range of events.

The aim of this book is to encourage better teaching of all the track events by school teachers, Assistant Club Coaches and Club Coaches. Effective and proper instruction in the Primary School and in the early years at the Secondary School is vital if the sport of Athletics is to have a solid foundation.

Teachers of beginners, both in school and in the athletics club, must realise that the skills, equipment, facilities and competitions associated with the Olympic Games and other such tournaments are not necessarily those required by the novice athlete. The learner requires the fundamentals of sound event technique, sufficient for improvement and enjoyment. Equipment and facilities should be adequate for the novice to learn skills safely and easily. The demand of competition is that it should sufficiently motivate the beginner to participate further in the sport of athletics.

Malcolm Arnold B.A.F. *National Coach, Wales*

CONTENTS

CHAPTER 1

THE BASICS

TEACHING TECHNIQUES

It is important to know how to teach technique efficiently. It is not sufficient to have been a good performer in order to teach technique properly. The coach must have a sound understanding of the techniques of running, hurdling and relay running. He must also understand the capabilities of his athletes, so that the level of instruction relates to their particular stage of development. Novice athletes must be taught technique well, under expert tuition. A point worth remembering is that when groups become too large, the expertise of the coach or teacher is diluted. It is best, when possible, to keep groups small so that individual attention can be given.

PRACTICAL AIDS TO LEARNING TECHNIQUES

Visual Aids

The use of visual aids is very important. Children are usually very good mimics and one should make use of this quality. A large amount of what we learn is through visual stimuli. Therefore, correct demonstration is vital. Use photographs, films, television performances and live action to aid the teaching of correct techniques.

Verbal Guidance

It is important to distinguish between encouragement and proper verbal guidance! Whatever is said to a group of athletes must be concise, positive, encouraging and to the point. Coaches and teachers usually talk too much and the essence of instruction can be lost in a welter of confusing words. Beware of the use of athletics terminology and jargon with beginner athletes. Always make sure that the athlete understands what has been said.

Manual Guidance

This type of guidance refers to the placement of limbs into technically correct positions; it can often be used when words fail, or even before words fail!

General Points on Technical Instruction

1. Children are most adept at learning techniques between eight and thirteen years of age.
2. When teaching techniques, consider only one technical point at a time.
3. Place technical training before fitness training in a session.
4. Technical work should not continue for more than 20 minutes without a break.
5. Practices devised for technical training [e.g. individual skills, drills etc.] must be directly related to the event.

6. When introducing a new technique, it will probably be helpful to modify the rules initially, in order to further the aims of technique training. For example, the height of the hurdles and/or the distance between the hurdles could be reduced.
7. Remember that the learning of a new skill must be enjoyable for the athlete. The coach and teacher must use reasonable praise as a means of motivation.

Competition

Competition can provide great motivation for some athletes.For others it can be a negative stimulus. It is important that young athletes are actually taught techniques which have subsequently become quite stable before competition is allowed. Secondly, within the rules of athletics, it is possible to allow young athletes to compete in higher age groups. Coaches, teachers and anxious, over ambitious parents should always think carefully before pitching their physically precocious young performers into a higher grade of athletics. Sometimes this experience can be stimulating and rewarding to the youngster. On the other hand it can be a very damaging experience psychologically. Often the young athlete does not recover from such experiences and is lost to athletics. It is best to allow young athletes to develop within their own age group. Remember that athletics can offer many types of competition.

Try the following:-
1. Competing against one another.
2. The athlete alone against the stop watch or the tape measure.
3. The athlete alone against his previous best time or distance.
4. The athlete versus the Five Star or Ten Step Award Charts [in England and Wales] or the Thistle Award Charts [Scotland]. Remember that none of these fine award schemes is a substitute for teaching athletics. Before anyone is tested in an event, the event must first be taught!
5. The preceding four points are objective methods of assessing athletic performance. Subjective judgement should be used where there is technical improvement. Although athletes do not score points for technical excellence, like gymnasts or skaters, always express approval for good technical performance.

UNDERSTANDING YOUNG ATHLETES

There is a great danger in assuming that young athletes are scaled down versions of senior athletes. It is quite wrong to devise a training schedule for a group of twelve year old athletes which is half the schedule given to a 24 year old mature athlete! Some of the physiological and developmental features of young people are mentioned here as a key to the type of work best suited to them. Further information on these topics is available in the B.A.F. publications "Training Theory" and "Assistant Club Coach Manual."

The Young Athlete - Some Aspects of Growth

This process begins in the womb and concludes between the ages of 18 and 22 years. Moderate and well executed training exercises have a positive effect on growth. Bones of greater cross section and higher tensile strength are produced. There is a pre-pubertal growth spurt, which on average begins at 9 years and reaches its peak at 11 years in girls. With boys it begins at 11 years and reaches its peak at 14 years. Bone growth precedes muscular development, causing problems of co-ordination. Growth is also a fatiguing process, which implies longer periods of rest between and within training sessions.

With running activities, preference should be given to steady running over longer distances and to fast running over short distances, with adequate recovery periods. As a general rule young athletes should not be put and kept in deep oxygen debt by using fast runs with very short recovery periods.

ATHLETICS
COACH

The Coaching Journal of the B.A.F.

Published:
March, June, September, December

Details from:
Malcolm Arnold
56 Rolls Avenue
Penpedairheol
Hengoed, Mid Glam. CF8 8HQ

CHAPTER 2

THE ORGANISATION OF GROUPS

The coach in the local athletics club will have more time to devote to the teaching of athletics than the school teacher, especially if he is committed to an all year round training programme. Whatever the situation, teaching sessions should contain the following elements:

- Each session must have a formal beginning and end.

- Athletes should be properly dressed, having regard for both cleanliness and the prevailing climatic conditions.

- Teacher or coach should also be properly dressed for the situation, having regard for the standards and examples to be set.

- Training/Teaching sessions must be planned in advance, within an overall scheme used by the club or school.

- Each session must have an aim, as well as a realistic and achievable objective, for each athlete taking part in the session.

The following format is suggested for each training session or lesson; the length of each part depends upon the total time available.

A warm up

Mobility exercises - general

Mobility exercises - specific to an event or a particular part of the body

Technical training

Fitness training

A warm down

In greater detail, each element should contain the following:-

WARM UP
This is a preparation for work to be done. It is usually

a. Physiological, where the broad aims are:-
   i) the generation of bodily warmth, in readiness for mobility exercises
   ii) the raising of muscle temperature, to ensure more efficient muscular contraction.

5

b. The rehearsal and practice of skills previously learned. This aspect is very important in pre-competition warm up routine.

MOBILITY EXERCISES

These exercises are done to increase the range of movement in a joint or a series of joints. If an athlete has supple muscles and flexible joints, he is able to apply force through a greater range of movement. As an example, stride length in sprinting is influenced by hip mobility. He can also achieve proper and efficient hurdle clearance positions.

Mobility work is a very important element in the training of young athletes. Begin with general exercises and develop these into exercises specific to an event. Mobility exercises relevant to the runner and the hurdler are shown in figures 1 to 11. These are mainly for the lower back, the hip joints and the legs. The BAF book "Mobility Training" gives further details and advice on the many types of exercise that can be done.

Fig. 1

Fig. 2a

Fig. 2b

Fig. 3a

Fig. 3b

Fig. 4a

Fig. 4b

Fig. 5

Fig. 6

Fig. 7

Fig. 8

Fig. 9a

Fig. 9b

Fig. 10a

Fig. 10b

Fig. 11

TECHNICAL TRAINING

This part of the session will be most important for the young athlete, where aims such as "teaching the standing start" or "teaching hurdling" will be pursued.

FITNESS TRAINING

This part of the training session should always follow the technical training. This is because young athletes need to be physically fresh to undertake technical training. Here the athlete can undertake activities designed to improve SPEED, STAMINA, or STRENGTH, or a combination of those qualities.

WARM DOWN

Sessions should always have a proper conclusion. Never allow athletes to drift away in an aimless fashion. The following activities are examples of how a session can be properly concluded:-

• Jog a certain distance, followed by a formal dispersal of the group.

• Call the athletes together and evaluate progress [or lack of it!] during the session.

• Give instructions for the next session.

• Outline the objectives to be achieved before the next session - e.g. the athletes may have to train on their own for one or two sessions until they see the coach or teacher during the following week.

• Whet the appetite of the athletes by telling them what will be done in the next training session.

The teacher or coach must ensure that every session or lesson is well organised and conducted, through proper discipline, motivation and good group organisation.

THE SAFETY OF ATHLETES

Coaches and teachers must always ensure the safety of the group in their charge and also have regard for others using athletics facilities. At an athletics track people of all ages are practising a variety of events. Serious accidents will happen if safety is disregarded. The following points, whilst not exhaustive, will help to ensure the safety of athletes.

On the track:-
- Instil good lane discipline.
- Warm up in the outside lanes.
- Be aware that athletes will be running very fast in the inner lanes.
- Do not stand talking on the track - you will inconvenience others.
- Remember that synthetic and grass surfaces are slippery in wet conditions.
- The infield is usually only for throwers - remind athletes about the procedure for

crossing the infield, so that they will not run into or be struck by throwing implements.

On the road:-
- Running on roads should be avoided whenever possible.
- If athletes must run on the road, remind them to run against the`grain'of traffic and not with it, so that they can see the oncoming traffic.
- Footpaths should be used whenever possible.
- "See and be seen" - when running at night, wear light coloured clothing. Better still, wear clothing which has luminous strips sewn into it. Devise running circuits which are lit by pavement lights.

Cross Country:-
- If possible, coaches should run round the course beforehand and then warn athletes of any hidden dangers which might be apparent on the course.
- If the weather is wet and cold, ensure that the athletes can get showered and changed quickly.
- Do not allow children to run in very extreme weather conditions.

Hurdling:-
- Never hurdle on wet grass or other slippery surfaces.
- Never allow athletes to cross a hurdle the "wrong" way.
- Ensure that hurdles are well maintained.

There are many other safety rules which will apply in your locality. Teachers should check their own Local Education Authority rules and clubs who hire school gymnasiums should do likewise. A leaflet entitled "Athletics - Keep It Safe" is available from the BAF, EDGBASTON HOUSE, 3 DUCHESS PLACE, HAGLEY ROAD, EDGBASTON, BIRMINGHAM, B16 8NM, price 50 pence per copy including post and packing. It can be unfolded to form an A2 size poster which is suitable for display on school and club notice boards.

CHAPTER THREE

THE RUNNING EVENTS

All runners, both sprinters and middle distance runners, must aim to improve their running speed. The ability to run fast over either short or long distances has its roots in hereditary factors, but a lot can be done by acquiring a more efficient running technique and higher levels of physical fitness.

Youngsters must be encouraged to run freely with a smooth and fast action. The following points of technique should be introduced to the beginner:-

- The LEGS propel the body forwards.
  They move in a cyclic manner through the following phases

  - SUPPORT [figure 12]
  - DRIVE [figure 13]
  - RECOVER [figure 14]

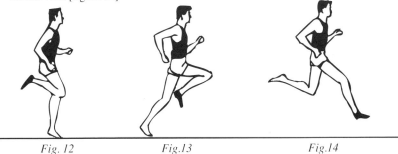

| Fig. 12 | Fig.13 | Fig.14 |

Novices should be made aware of the quickness and lightness of the running action and of the driving action of the leg, as in figure 13.
- The ARMS synchronise with the legs but work as opposites.
  - as the right leg is in its driving phase, the left elbow is driving backwards [figure 13]
  - as the right leg recovers, so the left arm recovers to a position in front of the trunk.
- The ARMS also balance the body, by absorbing the strong drive of the legs. Try running with the arms clasped behind the back - not for too long though!
- The ARMS should rotate on the shoulders in a backwards/forwards movement.
- The ARMS should swing parallel to the lane lines on the track, sometimes slightly across the body [especially in middle distance running].
- The ARMS also aid the force of the legs, when the foot is in contact with the ground [figure 13].
  Please note that the emphasis in the arm action should be the driving back of the elbows. As the elbows drive backwards, ask for a ninety degree angle to be kept at the elbow

Fig. 15

Fig. 16

Fig. 17   Fig. 18   Fig. 19

joint [figure 13]. Actually, the angle at the elbow opens out beyond ninety degrees at a certain stage in the running action, but asking for a ninety degree angle will produce the correct effect.

- The SHOULDERS should be kept still and square to the lane lines on the track.

MODIFICATIONS IN THE RUNNING ACTION

There are some sprinters who have the classical long striding action. This type of action is typified by the complete extension of the rear leg at the conclusion of the driving phase. Other sprinters have a quicker action, where the driving leg leaves the ground before it is fully extended. Very often the styles used are natural sprinting techniques. Usually, it is best to coach and enhance the style which comes most naturally to a sprinter.

As the distance the athlete runs increases, there is a greater need for running efficiency and economy. To compare the two extremes, a marathon runner cannot use the same exaggerated action as the sprinter. The distance runner is obliged to conserve energy in the following ways:-

- he will have a less vigorous leg drive
- he will have a lower and slower recovery from the leg drive
- he will have a less exaggerated arm action.

The arms will tend to swing more across the body. In extreme cases, the arms and shoulders will move in one unit.

POSTURE

Although there have been notable exceptions, most good runners have an erect posture with the head held in natural alignment with the spine. All extraneous head movements must be discouraged. The muscles of the face, jaw and shoulders must always be relaxed. The hips must be properly aligned under the trunk, with neither the bottom stuck out nor the hips unduly thrust forwards.

STARTING THE RACE

In events of short duration, there is a need for high starting efficiency. For example, a loss of half a second at the start of a 100 metre sprint would spell disaster. The loss of half a second by a 10,000 metres runner in the same situation could be made up. However, it is still important that distance runners are taught to start efficiently.

THE STARTING COMMANDS

For races up to and including 400 metres, the starting commands are:-
  - ON YOUR MARKS
  - SET
  - BANG
For races longer than 400 metres, the starting commands are:-
  - ON YOUR MARKS
  - BANG
By the rules of athletics, athletes must be motionless on the mark before the starter can proceed to the next command. Similarly, athletes must be motionless in the set position before the starter can fire the gun.

Good discipline is required from athletes when they are starting a race. Coaches and teachers will do a valuable job if they teach starting properly. Never encourage athletes to anticipate or beat the gun.

Please read the relevant rules in the B.A.F. handbook for a fuller description of all procedures relating to starting.

TYPES OF START
The Standing Start
The standing start should be taught to all beginners [figures 15 and 16]. In competition it is used exclusively for middle and long distance races. Novices may never progress further than the standing start, because they will find this the most effective way of starting. Advantages in using this type of start are:-

- The foot is placed up to the starting line [never on the line, which is against the rules]. Thus, the athlete is actually nearer the finish line, when compared with the crouch start.
- The arms are in position to synchronise immediately with the legs, following the report of the pistol. In the crouch start, both hands are placed up to the start line [figures 19 & 20]. Thus one arm will be out of phase. Some athletes have great difficulty in getting this out of phase arm back into proper synchronisation from the crouch start.
- It is easy to teach the discipline of a standing start.

Fig. 20

Fig. 21

Fig. 22

14

Teaching the Standing Start

1. Explain the rules of the standing start and the starting commands. Discourage the practice of trying to beat or anticipate the gun.

2. Organise the group into teams of three. Assemble them, one behind the other in lanes, 5 metres from the actual start line.

3. Give the command "On your marks". When the first group of athletes reach the start line, emphasise the following:-
   - Put the front foot up to the line [not on it].
   - Place the feet about shoulder width apart [30 to 50 centimetres] to obtain a good balanced position [figure15].
   - Obtain final balance by placing two thirds of the weight on the front foot and one third of the weight on the rear foot. Athletes will over balance if too much weight is placed on the front foot.
   - Bend the knees and lean forwards, with the arms properly synchronised with the legs [figure 16]. Whichever foot is placed at the line, the opposite arm will be forward.
   - Check the "on your marks" position thoroughly with each group of athletes.
   - When the "set" command is given, the athlete should bend the knees, stand motionless and concentrate on the report of the gun [figure 16]. In races over 400 metres, the athlete assumes this "set" position when the "on your marks" command is given.
   - Test the efficiency of the standing start by having competitions up to 50 metres.

Teaching the Crouch Start

The crouch start [figures 20-22] is a more complex technique than the standing start, but it can be learned easily by novices. It is pointless doing a crouch start if it is less efficient in competition than the standing start. Beginners and improvers are often better with the standing start.

The crouch start can be taught as a basic drill, using the same type of group organisation as for the standing start.

1. Give the command "on your marks". As the athletes reach the start line, give the following instructions:-
   - place the right foot behind the line.
   - place the left foot behind the right [figure 17].
   - remove the right foot from that position and place the right knee adjacent to the left ankle. The toe of the right foot should be turned under [figure 18]. This will give a distance between the feet of approximately one shin length and will place the front foot the correct distance away from the start line.

15

2. In the "on your marks" position, check the following:
    - the hands should be slightly wider than shoulder width apart viewed from the front [figure 19].
    - the fingers should form a bridge, with the thumbs pointing towards one another [figure 19]
    - When viewed from the side, the shoulders should be above the start line, not beyond it [figure 20]
    - the head should be in natural alignment with the spine [figure 20]. N.B. the athlete's fingers must be behind the line and not on it as shown in this photograph.

3. Once the "on your marks" position has been checked, move to the "set" position. Ask the athlete to lift the hips to a position slightly higher than shoulder level [figure 21].

Check the following points when the athlete reaches this position.

    - there should be a 90 degree angle at the front knee. There should be an angle of approximately 120 degrees at the rear knee [figure 21].

    - shoulders should still be above the start line [figure 21]. Coaches and teachers should try to develop a coaching eye, so that these positions can be recognised and quickly checked in the practical situation.

4. When the drills of going to the"on your marks" and "set" positions have been taught [this process should not take too long], go through the whole procedure of starting in the competitive situation.
    Whilst the athletes are competing, observe the following so that further improvements in sprinting technique can be effected:
    - Look at the head, neck and shoulders for any undue strain and tension.
    - Look at the position of the hips in relation to the shoulders [figure 21].
    - Look at the angles behind the knees [figure 21]. The back leg must not be straight and the toes of the back foot must be tucked under [figure 21].
    - Look at the synchronisation of the arms and legs. Remember that the arms and legs work as opposites. If the left leg is forward at the start, this will be the prime driving force. Therefore, the right arm will be driving backwards.
    - Examine the effectiveness of the crouch start. If the athlete first stands up straight after the gun fires, then begins to run forwards, reversion to the standing start might be the answer. If the athlete is potentially a very good sprinter, then the process of coaching a skilled crouch start is well worth pursuing [figure 22].

The starting position that has been described is often called a "medium start". This "medium" description refers to the distance between the front foot and the line, and the distance between the feet in the "on your marks" and "set" positions. Teachers and coaches might wish to experiment further and try modifications of this "medium" start.

- Alter the front foot position in relation to the starting line for "feel" and for comfort.
- Try a wider spacing between the feet [i.e. greater than shin length].
- Try a narrower spacing [i.e. less than shin length].

HINTS ON DEVELOPING SPEED

1. Running speed can be developed in four ways:
   - by moving the limbs faster
   - by increasing the length of each stride
   - by improving endurance, so that athletes can sustain their top speed longer
   - by learning to relax at speed.
2. Before speed training begins, there is a need for good physical conditioning.
3. There should be minimal fatigue in pure speed running [as distinct from speed endurance training].
4. Pure speed is developed when working at 75% to 100% of maximum running speed. There are occasions when athletes in longer distance events are running faster than their racing speed.
5. Maximum speed is achieved after 5 to 6 seconds of running, earlier with younger athletes.

COMPETITIVE SPRINTING

The running and starting techniques that are taught to novice athletes should eventually stand the test of competition. Races over short distances which do not involve too much endurance will make an adequate test, as will shuttle and continuous relays.

ENDURANCE RUNNING

In the teaching of endurance running, we in Britain work from a position of great strength. There is a very strong tradition of cross country and other forms of endurance running. There are large numbers of endurance runners and the quality of performance is very high. There are excellent facilities for endurance training and competition using the roads, fields, woods, beaches and hills.

BASIC PRINCIPLES

Physiologists tell us that the most efficient way to run longer distances is at an even pace. In this situation, the oxygen uptake of an athlete meets oxygen demands. When the oxygen supply does not meet those demands, an oxygen deficiency occurs and the athlete "runs out of breath". When an athlete incurs this oxygen debt, he must either reduce speed or stop and rest. In a race, even paced running is rarely possible all the time, because the tactics of other individuals in the race will dictate otherwise. However, even paced running is a very important principle to learn and is basic to endurance running.

Once even paced running has been learned, teaching and training will be geared to an improvement of:
- oxygen uptake
- running technique.

It must be noted that the majority of work done with youngsters will be either steady state running or speed running, where the athlete runs fast over shorter distances and is allowed to recover before beginning the next repetition. The temptation to do intensive "anaerobic" oxygen debt tolerance training must be resisted until the athlete begins to mature in the late teens.

Neil Armstrong, Director of the Physical Education Association Research Centre at Exeter University, has suggested the following aerobic training prescription for young athletes:

FREQUENCY   3 to 5 times per week
INTENSITY   75% - 90% of maximal heart rate *
TIME   20 - 40 minutes at the above rate

• If you are unable to determine maximal heart rate, assume a value of 210 beats per minute for children and 200 for adolescents.

SUGAR THE PILL

Sometimes, teachers and coaches of young people need to be confidence givers. Endurance running can be a difficult pill to swallow for the less able athlete. If a youngster's introduction to middle distance running happens on a wet, freezing November day, wearing only a vest and a pair of shorts and flimsy canvas shoes, the desire to return to the sport in the future will be diminished!

Endurance running can be monotonous for the young athlete and monotony dulls the spirit. The following are some activity suggestions which will help to sugar the pill.

1. Begin with steady running over short distances in fine weather.If this climatic requirement cannot be met, ensure that athletes are adequately clothed for the prevailing weather conditions.

2. Use handicap ratings. Run around a short course for a time. Then establish handicap ratings within a group. Thus if Frank runs one minute faster than Dave, then Frank will start the next run one minute later than Dave. This means that athletes of all abilities will

have incentive and motivation in each handicap run.

3. Relay Running. Run a relay over [for example] laps of a field, with teams of three, four or five athletes running one or two laps each. Evenly balanced teams can be selected from handicap times.

4. Devil take the hindmost. This activity favours the best runners in the group. The athlete who is last as the group passes given points on the track must drop out of the event.

5. Paarlauf - this is a word meaning pair running - two athletes doing a continuous relay for a set distance, or for a set time, over a pre-determined course.

6. Flag Runs. Flags are put out at certain intervals [say 130 metres, 135 metres, 140 metres, 145 metres and 150 metres] from the start line. A standard of 20 seconds is set [which will vary according to the standard of athlete]. If the athlete reaches the 150 metre flag in 20 seconds, he is awarded 5 points, and so on, down to 1 point for reaching the 130 metres flag. A two minute jog back recovery is allowed between runs. The athlete who scores the most points over a set number of runs is the winner.

7. Beat the Clock. The athlete runs fast for 15 seconds, 30 seconds, 60 seconds and 90 seconds, with a 3 minute rest between runs. The distance achieved is then marked. The athlete rests for 10 minutes, and then runs for the same length of time again - 15, 30, 60 and 90 seconds, and tries to run further than the first set of distances achieved.

CHAPTER FOUR

THE RELAYS

Relay running is a most enjoyable form of training and competition. Teams must be taught well and an "esprit de corps" encouraged.

Relay events fall into three broad categories.

SHUTTLE RELAYS
These are done by teams being selected from the group or class. Each team is then divided into two and its members positioned so that they face each other at a set distance apart.

For example, if there are six in a team, numbers one, three and five stand at one end of the course and numbers two, four and six stand at the other end. The first athlete is then given the starting command and the teams shuttle run back and forth. Each relay runner sets off the next in his team by a touch of hands or by passing on the relay baton. The race can last for as long as the coach or teacher determines, e.g. the race could continue until every athlete has had three runs.

OUT AND BACK RELAYS
In this type of relay, groups are divided into teams and set out behind a starting line. Objects, such as bean bags or footballs - in fact anything easily carried by the athlete - are set out at points equidistant from the start line. The first runner then brings back the objects individually and places them in a bucket, e.g. at the starting line. When all the objects are collected by the first runner, the second runner replaces them back in their original positions one by one. Then the third runner brings them back individually - and so on until the relay is completed.

RELAY EVENTS ON THE TRACK
The usual track relays are:-
  - 4 x 100 metres relay
  - 4 x 400 metres relay

Other recognised relays are sometimes contested but are not part of the standard track programme. These are:-
- 4 x 200 metres relay
- 4 x 800 metres relay
- 4 x 1500 metres relay
- Medley relay [200 metres + 200 metres + 400 metres + 800 metres]

In schools and clubs, the distances run and the number of athletes per team can be varied to suit the occasion and the age and ability of the athletes.

The circular relay on the track involves passing a relay baton as efficiently and quickly as possible. In the 4 x 100 metres relay, the baton is passed from the incoming runner to the outgoing runner in the relay zone. The relay take-over zone is shown in figure 23.

There are three relay zones around the 400 metres track. The mid lines of each of these zones are exactly 100 metres apart. The runner who receives the baton [i.e. the outgoing runner] may run and accelerate in the acceleration zone, BUT the baton may only change hands between the incoming and outgoing runners in the twenty metre take-over zone [refer again to figure 23].

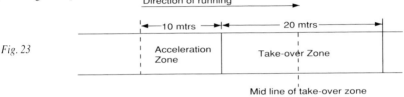

Fig. 23

The baton must be carried in the hand throughout the race and may not be thrown!

If the baton is dropped, it must be recovered by the athlete who dropped it. The passing of the baton is complete at the moment it is in the hand of the outgoing runner only.

Within the take-over zone, it is only the position of the baton which is decisive and not the positions of either the bodies or limbs of the athletes.

4 x 100 METRES RELAY

There are four runners carrying and passing one relay baton through three changes. It is only the baton which travels the full 400 metres. Therefore, the speed matching and baton passing between the two runners at each take-over zone is very critical. Essentially, a high baton speed must be maintained throughout the race.

There are a number of alternative methods of exchanging a relay baton. The Alternate Upsweep change is probably the easiest method to learn and is also the safest. With beginners, there is probably no need to use the acceleration zones, as they reach top speed quite quickly. This also reduces the distance young athletes have to run. Thus they do not become fatigued quite so quickly.

Fig. 24

Fig. 25

21

NON VISUAL CHANGES

The best sprint relay changes are non-visual. This means that the outgoing runner watches the incoming runner on to a check mark. He then turns and accelerates towards top speed without looking back again at the incoming runner or the baton. This ensures that the outgoing runner sprints smoothly and does not run sideways as a result of looking back [figure 24].

Fig. 26a

ALTERNATE HANDS

By using the alternate hands method, the outgoing runner does not change the baton from one hand to the other after receiving it. The first runner will carry the baton in the right hand. The second stands on the outside of the lane and receives the baton in the left hand. The third runner stands on the inside of the lane and receives the baton in the right hand. Finally, the fourth runner stands on the outside of the lane and receives the baton in the left hand.

THE UPSWEEP BATON PASS

This method is called the upsweep simply because the baton, as it is put into the receiver's hand, is swept up from below the hand.

As the incoming runner reaches the outgoing runner in the take-over zone, he must give a verbal signal so that the outgoing runner knows precisely when to present the hand for the baton. He can shout "hand" or "now", or whatever is thought to be most reliable. Preferably, we do not want a situation where all eight teams enter a relay zone - neck and neck- and all the teams shout "hand". This could be very confusing for the outgoing runners!

As the verbal signal is shouted, the outgoing runner must present his hand ready to receive the baton [figure 25]. Once the receiving hand is in position, the incoming runner puts the baton into the hand in a positive manner. He must make sure that the baton is placed correctly into the hand [figure 25], so that there is plenty of baton to give to the next runner. If not enough baton is given, the receiving runner must push the baton through his hand, usually by pressing it against the thigh. Needless to say, this slows the runner.

THE DOWNSWEEP BATON PASS

This method is so called, because the baton, when placed into the receiver's hand, is swept down on to the upturned palm [figure 26a]. When the verbal signal is given to the outgoing runner, he stretches the arm back, parallel to the ground with the palm upturned. The end of the baton is placed onto the palm of the receiver. With the downsweep method, compared with the upsweep, a greater distance between runners can be achieved at the moment of exchange, which is desirable [figure 26b].

Fig. 26b

SPEED MATCHING

It has already been established that baton speed throughout a relay race is vital. Ideally, the incoming and outgoing runners should be at their fastest running speed as the baton is exchanged. If the baton is exchanged too early, the outgoing runner will still be accelerating to top speed. If the exchange is too late, then the incoming runner will probably be decelerating and the baton could change hands outside the take-over zone. A checkmark is placed on the track, so that accurate speed matching can take place. The outgoing runner is responsible for the placement of the checkmark, which is established after a number of rehearsal runs. The checkmark is placed correctly if the baton pass takes place between 12 and 16 metres from the beginning of the take-over zone [figure 27].

Fig. 27

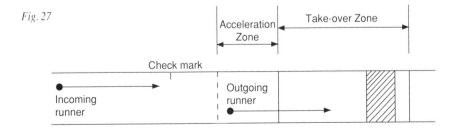

During practice runs, start with the checkmark placed at 25 lengths of the outgoing runner's feet. If the incoming runner catches the outgoing runner too early in the take-over zone, the checkmark must be adjusted to a distance greater than 25 foot lengths. If the incoming runner does not catch the outgoing runner, then the check mark must be adjusted to a distance less than 25 foot lengths.

Fig. 28

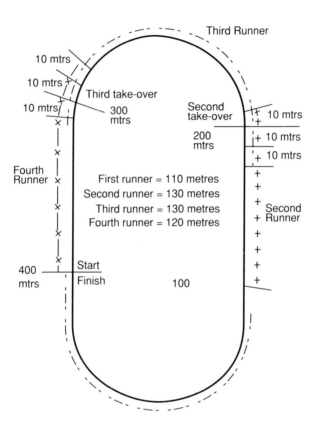

First runner = 110 metres
Second runner = 130 metres
Third runner = 130 metres
Fourth runner = 120 metres

SELECTION OF RELAY RUNNERS
When selecting runners for a sprint relay team, many factors are considered.

1. SPEED
   Ideally, the four fastest runners should be chosen for a relay team, but the following points should also be considered.

2. *RELIABILITY*

The athletes chosen must be reliable in:-
- Starting their outgoing run when the incoming runner passes the check mark. If the outgoing runner starts early or late, the check mark loses its significance.
- Presenting the hand properly, to receive the baton from the incoming runner.
- Giving the verbal signal to the outgoing runner at the correct time.
- Giving the baton to the outgoing runner in the correct manner.

3. *FACTORS OF DISTANCE*

As can be seen in figure 28, the various legs of the relay differ from each other, both in distance and in character. In this example, using the acceleration zones:-
- The first runner travels 110 metres, runs mainly on the bend, must be a good starter and must be good at passing the baton.
- The second runner travels 130 metres, runs mainly on the straight, and must be a good receiver and passer of the baton.
- The third runner travels 130 metres, runs mainly on the bend, and must also be a good receiver and passer of the baton.
- The fourth runner travels 120 metres, runs mainly on the straight, and must be a good receiver of the baton.

By varying the point at which the outgoing runner starts running, the distance that each runner covers can be altered. With young athletes whose sprinting speed is relatively low, by not using the acceleration zones the distances of the second, third and fourth legs can be reduced by ten metres each.

ACTIVITIES FOR TEACHING BATON PASSING

Baton passing activities should be taught early, preferably in the eight to thirteen years old age span. At these ages, children are very receptive to skill learning and will enjoy relay skills and competitions.

Static Baton Passing

a) Place athletes in groups of four, one in front of the other, about one metre apart, with one relay baton per group.
b) Teach the method of presenting the arm and the hand to receive the baton for the upsweep change, as in figure 25.
c) Teach the method of giving the baton. Figure 25 shows the correct method. Essentially, the giving runner should put plenty of baton into the receiving runner's hand, so that there is plenty of baton to give to the next runner down the line.

Fig. 29

Fig. 30

d) Explain the method of the alternate change and place the athletes so that alternate passing can take place, as in figure 29. Runner 1 holds the baton in the right hand and passes to the left hand of runner 2, and so on down the line.

e) After these early teaching stages, the runners present their receiving hands and the baton is passed down the line in a slick manner.

f) The next stage of instruction includes verbal signals. The giving runner calls "hand", or whatever signal is decided upon. The receiving runner presents the hand and the baton is passed. At this stage, there is a danger of the giving runner trying to pass the baton as the call is made and before the receiving hand is presented. Specifically, the pattern is:-

- SHOUT
- PRESENT THE HAND
- PLACE THE BATON INTO THE RECEIVING HAND

g) Once these skills have been learned, the situation can develop by doing baton passing in groups of four whilst jogging.

26

h) Baton passing must now be learned in the take-over zones. The most important aspects are:-
   - the establishment of checkmarks.
   - the establishment of baton pass at the highest running speed and at the correct take-over point in the zone.

i) At each stage of learning the baton pass, be it static passing or running passing, the coach should put the skill to the test in a competitive situation.

BATON PASSING WHEN RUNNERS ARE VERY FATIGUED

In running events where fatigue is a major factor, for example in the 4 x 400 metres relay, the method of passing the baton is modified from the non-visual sprint method. The modification is made because the change is made between a very fresh outgoing runner and a very fatigued incoming runner. The outgoing runner must judge the state of the incoming runner and adjust the pace of his start accordingly. The method of change recommended is shown in figure 30 where:-

1. The incoming runner holds the baton out in the right hand.

2. The outgoing runner:-
   - uses a visual method
   - holds out the left hand
   - judges the speed and fatigue of the incoming runner
   - takes the baton from the incoming runner in an authoritative manner
   - immediately changes the baton over to the right hand, ready for the next change.

This type of change can be used for the longer relays on the track, for example 4 x 400 metres and medley relays, and for cross country relays, road relays or continuous relays.

CHAPTER FIVE

THE HURDLING EVENTS

Hurdling is rhythmic sprinting over obstacles which are placed in a regular pattern on the track. Hurdling always compromises the athlete's natural sprinting action because of the following three main factors:-

1. The hurdle height for a particular age group is constant [see table on page 34].

2. The distance between hurdles for a particular age group is constant.

3. The RELATIVE effect of the height of the hurdle and the distance between hurdles varies according to the ability of each athlete, particularly with:-
   - the athlete's sprinting speed
   - the athlete's length of leg.

The athlete's physical characteristics determine the degree of the compromise. These problems of compromise particularly affect the teaching of hurdling to beginners. It is important to help the athletes in the learning situation, by lowering the hurdles and altering the distance between hurdles. The hurdling grid [figure 31] with its many alternatives, is vital to the teaching of hurdling. By using the grid, a child can be matched to the group of hurdles suitable to his or her stature.

TEACHING SPRINT HURDLING

The first principle to establish is the stride pattern to the first hurdle and the stride pattern between the hurdles. Most athletes take 8 strides to the first hurdle. Other very able and long legged athletes can take 7 strides to the first hurdle. All athletes should take 3 strides between each hurdle.

Teaching Activities
Set up low benches, or canes and skittles, so that the class can take three strides between each obstacle. Ignore obstacle clearance techniques, but encourage an uninterrupted sprint pattern over and between them. Do not put benches on top of each other to simulate hurdle height - it is very dangerous.

Set up hurdles outdoors at the lowest possible height. Using the three stride pattern between hurdles, encourage rhythmic sprinting over and between the hurdles.

SAFETY NOTE: Hurdling is dangerous on wet grass or any other slippery surface. It is also dangerous for children to run over hurdles in the opposite way to the correct running direction [i.e. with the feet of the hurdles on the far side].

Fig. 31

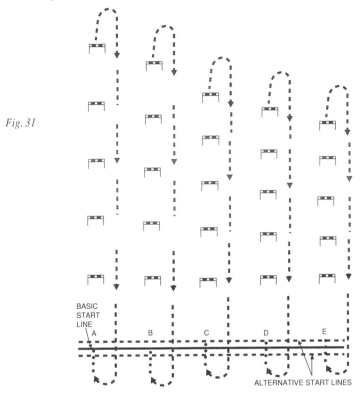

Hurdle Clearance

Hurdlers should aim to clear their obstacles as quickly and efficiently as possible, raising their centre of gravity only a little more than in a normal running stride. This is achieved by a running step-over action with the leading leg and a sideways trailing action with the rear leg.

The Leading Leg
- Must be picked up fast, bent at the knee [figure 32]
- As the flexed knee reaches barrier height, the heel is driven at the barrier [figures 33 & 34]
- As the leading heel passes the barrier, it is returned to the ground as quickly as possible [figures 35 & 36].

Fig. 32   Fig. 33   Fig. 34   Fig. 35   Fig. 36   Fig. 37

The Trailing Leg
- As the leading leg drives at the barrier, the trailing leg is still in contact with the ground, driving the body forwards [figure 33]
- When the trailing leg leaves the ground, it is swung to the side, flexed at the knee [figure 34]
- Think of the trailing knee as pulling the foot through after it, so that a full stride is taken off the hurdle [figures 35 - 37].

The Arms
The arms synchronise with the legs during barrier clearance and work as opposites. Efficient use of the arms enables the athlete to return to a sprinting action between the barriers as soon as possible.

HURDLE CLEARANCE TEACHING ACTIVITIES

Hurdle Walking
- Set up hurdles in a hurdling grid [figure 31].
- Walk to each hurdle, lift the lead leg over as described earlier and pull the trail leg over to the side.
- As the leading leg lands, concentrate on the trailing knee pulling the trailing foot through high into the next stride.

Hurdle Stepping
Have a space separating each flight of hurdles in the hurdling grid, so that athletes can walk or run down each side of the flight of hurdles [figure 31].

Fig. 39

Fig. 38

The Leading Leg

Isolate the leading leg by running down one side of the flight of hurdles. If the leading leg is the right leg, run down the left side of the hurdles [figure 38].

- Approach the hurdle with a high stepping action, quite slowly initially.
- As each hurdle is cleared, the action of the leg is isolated and can be examined and analysed carefully.
- As the level of skill improves, so the speed can be increased.

The Trailing Leg

The trailing leg can be isolated in similar fashion to the leading leg, by running down the other side of the hurdle [figure 39].

The following points should be encouraged:-

- a fast action of the knee
- the foot of the trailing leg being pulled through into the next stride.

Add the action of the lead leg and the trail leg, after isolating them, and examine the whole action.

Place the skill into a competitive situation at various stages through the learning process.

STARTING FOR HURDLING

The starting commands for hurdling events are exactly the same as for the sprinting events.

The standing start described in the sprinting section will be adequate for the hurdles events and, in many cases with the beginner athletes, more efficient than the crouch start. There is a marked difference between the crouch start for a hurdles event and a sprints event. When hurdling, the athlete must be prepared to clear the first obstacle some seven or eight strides after leaving the blocks. In sprinting, that athlete aims to drive hard in a low position for

31

some eight to ten strides after the start. When teaching a start for hurdling use the variable start line shown in the hurdling grid. Also, encourage the athlete to be up and looking to sight the hurdle for clearance after the fourth stride off the blocks.

400 METRES HURDLING

The scope of hurdling events has been widened for young athletes in recent years. Athletes can now run over 400 metres hurdles in the 15-17 and the 17-20 age groups. The 400 metres hurdles for women is now a fully recognised event in all major championships at schools and senior levels. The distances up to and between hurdles are exactly the same for all age groups.

From the start to the first hurdle	45 metres
Between each hurdle	35 metres
From the tenth hurdle to the finish	40 metres

The height of the hurdles varies between age groups.

All women's events	76.2.cms [2ft 6ins]
15-17 yrs	84 cms. [2ft 9ins]
Seniors and 17 - 20 years	91.4.cms [3ft]

It is useful for young athletes to have a grounding in sprint hurdling before beginning 400 metres hurdling. It is also useful to be able to use either leg as the lead leg. To be able to lead with either leg is called "alternating". This allows the athlete to use either an odd or even number of strides between hurdles during a race. An athlete needs to do this because the fatigue factor is high in the 400 metres hurdles. As the athlete runs the race, fatigue will set in after the fifth hurdle. As this occurs, the athlete will change down and use a greater number of strides between hurdles. If the athlete can alternate, the change down becomes a smoother and more natural progression.

It is important to understand stride patterns in 400 metres hurdling. The current world record holder, Ed Moses [U.S.A.], uses an almost unique stride pattern. He takes 20 strides to the first hurdle, 13 strides between each hurdle and 16 strides from the tenth hurdle to the finish line. Young athletes, beginning to learn the event, are likely to take 23 or 24 strides to the first hurdle and up to 18 or 19 strides between hurdles. As the athlete learns and improves, the number of strides up to the first hurdle and between hurdles will decrease.

Athletes must learn to run boldly between hurdles. Novices sometimes use three strides where two will do, but this slows the athlete and should be discouraged.

Some of the following activities will help the beginner 400 metre hurdler.

Hurdling Skill
In the following activities, the coach or teacher should experiment with hurdle spacings, so that athletes will run smoothly over and between hurdles.

1. To encourage alternating
   - 5 hurdles placed 4 strides apart
   - 5 hurdles placed 6 strides apart
   - Normal sprint hurdles drills, concentrating upon lead and trail leg, right and left.

2. To encourage good 400 metre hurdling
In the following exercises, the hurdles must be set at the correct 35 metre spacings. These exercises are done to produce correct stride patterns, smooth hurdling and good hurdles clearance.
   - run from the start to hurdle 1. If the athlete reaches hurdle 1 on the "wrong" leg, change the feet round at the start.
   - run from the start to hurdle 5.
   - run from the start to hurdle 8. Substantial fatigue will result from this run.
   - run over 10 hurdles to rehearse the pattern of the whole race. The athlete will also be very fatigued from this activity.

Hurdling Fitness
Top class adult athletes do a lot of hurdling fatigue exercises. This type of activity is not for youngsters. If young athletes go into oxygen debt, they should be allowed to recover fully before subsequent repetition.

Activities
   • Steady running, such as cross country, interval relay or fartlek during the winter.
   • Fast running, with repetitions over 40 metres, 80 metres, 150 metres and 200 metres.

Full recovery rests should be allowed after sprinting and hurdling repetitions.

SPECIFICATIONS FOR PARTICULAR HURDLE EVENTS ARE:

Distance of Race	Hurdle Height	Start to First Hurdle	Distance between Hurdles	Last Hurdle to Finish	No. of Hurdles
MENS EVENTS					
17 - 20 Years					
110M	99.0cm	13.72m	9.14m	14.02m	10
200M	76.2cm	18.29m	18.29m	17.1m	10
400M	91.4cm	45m	35m	40m	10
15 - 17 Years					
100M	91.4cm	13m	8.5m	10.5m	10
400M	84.0cm	45m	35m	40m	10
13 - 15 Years					
80M	84.0cm	12m	8m	12m	8
11 - 13 Years					
80M	76.2cm	12m	8m	12m	8

Distance of Race	Hurdle Height	Start to First Hurdle	Distance between Hurdles	Last Hurdle to Finish	No. of Hurdles
WOMENS EVENTS					
Senior & 17 - 20 Years					
100M	84.0cm	13m	8.5m	10.5m	10
400M	76.2cm	45m	35m	40m	10
15 - 17 Years					
80M	76.2cm	12m	8m	12m	8
100M	76.2cm	13m	8.5m	10.5m	10
200M	76.2cm	16m	19m	13m	10
300M	76.2cm	50m	35m	40m	7
400M	76.2cm	45m	35m	40m	10
13 - 15 Years					
75M	76.2cm	11.5m	7.5m	11m	8
11 - 13 Years					
70M	68.2cm	11m	7m	10m	8

APPENDIX

Some useful addresses:

The British Athletic Federation
Edgbaston House
3 Duchess Place
Hagley Road
Edgbaston
Birmingham B16 8NM
(Tel: 021 456 4050)

The Five Star Award Scheme is administered by the AAA of England at the above address.

The Thistle Award Scheme in Scotland, the equivalent of the Five Star Award Scheme, is administered from:
Caledonia House
South Gyle
Edinburgh EH12 9DQ.
(Tel:031 317 7323)

The Ten Step Award Scheme is aimed at the 8 - 10 age group, but many older children have found it challenging and enjoyable. It is administered throughout the U.K. by the South of England A.A. from their office at:
Suite 36
City of London Fruit Exchange
Brushfield Street
London E1 6EU
(Tel: 071 247 2963)

BAF publications can be ordered from:
BAF Athletics Bookcentre
5 Church Road
Great Bookham
Surrey KT23 3PN
(Tel: 0372 452 804)

NOTES